Tips for Teachers Teens

compiled by
KIM JACKSON

contributors
KIM JACKSON
JIM PIERSON
LYNN LUSBY PRATT
JANE L. SIMMONS

STANDARD
PUBLISHING
Cincinnati, Ohio

Edited by Karen Brewer
Illustrated by Keith Locke
Cover Illustration and Book Design by Sandy Wimmer

The Standard Publishing Company, Cincinnati, Ohio
A division of Standex International Corporation
© 1995 by The Standard Publishing Company
All rights reserved
Printed in the United States of America

02 01 00 99 98 97 96 95   5 4 3 2 1

Library of Congress Cataloging-in-Publication Data

Tips for teachers. Teens/compiled by Kim Jackson; contributors,
Kim Jackson, Jim Pierson.
     p.   cm.
   ISBN 0-7847-0317-5
   1. Christian education of teenagers. 2. Christian education-
-Teaching methods. I. Jackson, Kim. II. Pierson, Jim.
BV1485.T54   1995
268'.433--dc20
                                                      94-46747
                                                         CIP

CONTENTS

BUILDING RELATIONSHIPS

TEACHER/STUDENT

The single most important quality of great teachers is their care for each individual student.

Get-to-Know-the-Kids Vids **Make a short video clip of each of your students as a capsule of their interests and personality (i.e., in full football gear charging the camera, behind the counter at McDonalds). Each "vid" should begin with that kid holding a poster with his name, age, and school name. Use the videos to show on promotion Sunday, at youth parties, or to give to prospects with a title of "Meet the Kids From Our Church."**

That's Zoonika With a "K" **Learn the names (and proper spellings) of each of your students. Play a creative name game or let students design their own name tags to assist this process.**

First-Timer's Form **Ask each student (regulars and visitors alike) to fill out a form the first time they attend your class. Besides the usual name, age, church membership information, etc., include spaces for the student to list likes and dislikes, hobbies and talents. This form will give you insight into your students and is a wonderful tool for follow-up.**

Here's My Card Give each of your students one of your business cards or one from the church on which you have added your name and phone number. Even if they never use the card, the act shows you care.

Lights, Action, Eric! Focus in on your students' talents and interests and encourage them to pursue those gifts. Let's say Eric wants to be a movie producer. When an appropriate topic arises, say, "Hey Eric, maybe you could make your first blockbuster movie about this." Such a comment shows that you remember Eric's career dream and that you actually believe he can achieve it.

Brace Yourself for a Celebration When a student excitedly announces she's finally getting her braces off, for example, plan to serve caramel corn or some other braces-forbidden food. Tell your students, "The Bible says to 'Rejoice with those who rejoice,' so let's enjoy some caramel corn in honor of Stephanie's good news!"

The Early Bird Gets . . . To Know the Students Arrive early—but not to do any last minute lesson preparation. Go early and be available to visit with students as they arrive.

Safe Place Start creating an atmosphere of trust the first day of class. Inform students that you have no intention of humiliating them; they are free to ask questions and make comments; and you will not tolerate any negative "stuff" between students. This is a place where all members have the privilege of being comfortable.

The Dog Ate My Sunday School Lesson Be a real person to whom your students can relate. Teens will respond more positively to transparency and honesty than to perfectly pious people or seemingly super saints.

Star Search Plug in student talent *now!* Don't just encourage future careers. Ask your budding artist to create a class logo or illustrate a lesson. A young poet might write on a particular upcoming topic. Find ways to encourage and explore God-given gifts.

Welcome, Doubters Offer a safe environment for questions and doubts. Assure students that no angels with swords will appear to smite them if they say, "I'm not sure what I believe about this."

The Five-Eleven Principle—1 Thessalonians 5:11, That Is. Be an encourager. Kids tend to become what they are either encouraged or discouraged to become. Whether it be spoken or written, in the form of a handshake or a smile, subscribe to the 5:11 principle.

Three Little Words Don't be afraid of those three little words: "I don't know."

The Mobile Teacher Occasionally show up at students' non-church activities. Kids expect you to show up to teach, but to appear at a game, contest, pageant, or recital is an unexpected and encouraging "extra-mile" kind of thing.

Total Recall Your students may not remember all (or any!) of the lessons you teach, but rest assured, if you have loved them with the love of Jesus, they will remember *you.*

On the Other Hand . . . . If you are a great classroom teacher, but simply are unable to spend time with your students outside of class, don't sweat it. But check to see that youth sponsors or other adult leaders are filling this need.

Football Friday, Speech Team Saturday Call your students' schools to ask to get on their calendar-of-events mailing list. Many school booster clubs sell event calendars as well. If you aren't able to attend an event, you will at least know it's happening and you can refer to it.

Ha-Ha-Ha-O-Phobia If you want students to speak up in class, employ the artful use of their answers. Save students from incorrect answers, or they'll be too embarrassed to speak up again. You might say, "That is a popular opinion, but . . ." or "Yes, I just heard Oprah talking about that last week, and . . . ." Most answers will have at least a word you can work with. For fact questions, there's no way around a wrong answer—it's just plain wrong. But if you're creating an atmosphere of openness and acceptance, a little humor can help: "Well, I suppose Jesus could have met David on the road to Emmaus, except for one tiny detail—David had already been dead for several hundred years." Soon you'll find that the group can laugh out loud at the occasional offbeat reply without causing any pain.

Walk Down Memory Lane Talk to college age Christians and ask them what most impacted their lives for Jesus during their junior and senior high years. Then take a tip from someone who knows.

Be Real If you try too hard to be "cool," you'll just be weird! Be yourself, with just a dash of "cool" thrown in!

Building Relationships

Laugh Show your students that Christianity can be fun. It may never have occurred to them that the God who created the road runner and the chimpanzee may very well have a goofy streak!

Love 'Em or Leave 'Em If you don't *love* being with teens, maybe you should look for another area of service. But if you do love it, remember to tell them so.

In the Know Be informed about the world of today's teens. You don't have to know it all or like it all, but take time to find out what your students are watching, listening to, and reading.

Two Ears, One Mouth Listen. A good teacher is one whose ears get as much of a workout as his mouth.

God Don't Make No Junk Not every student is going to be the ideal: "normal," polite, intelligent, squeaky clean. But even the most . . . uh, bizarre teen is still God's creation, worthy of your best treatment and respect.

Bite Your Tongue Resist the urge to comment on "weird" hair, "ugly" clothes, and "stupid" music. These things are not important. Teaching kids what the Bible says, is.

Praying With Faces Keep a photo prayer journal. Ask each student to give you a school photograph (or take photos yourself) and place one photo on each page in your notebook. Then write prayer requests and praise reports by the appropriate student's photograph.

Rah, Rah! Recognize accomplishments. Post news clippings, programs, and photographs connected with your students' activities.

Tips for Teachers—Teens

Pray Pray for teens by name. And follow up on prayer needs and praise reports.

Hold Your Tongue Keep confidences.

Put Out the Welcome Mat Occasionally open your home to students.

Whadayathink? Ask teens for their opinions. Invite feedback. God may teach you something in the process!

Think Back Remember what it was like to be fourteen or seventeen? What was important to you? What qualified as "the end of the world?"

Handy Hallmark Keep a supply of postcards on hand. When a student makes a good point or has some astute comment, write two or three sentences on the card and mail it immediately. The smallest good deed is better than the greatest good intention.

High-Tech Devo Minute Leave a weekly creative devotional thought on your answering machine and tell students what hours they are allowed to call to hear it.

Follow-Up

Meet students where they are, not where you'd like them to be.

Quick and Easy Mail the day's work sheet or take-home paper to absentees so that the students get some idea of what was missed. Jot a "hope to see you next week" note on it before mailing.

Think Big Picture For long-range follow-up, keep a notebook of all the students you have taught. Jot down tidbits, funny comments they made in class, etc. Check up on your former students in a year, in five years. (This notebook makes a good prayer journal as well).

Information Highway Feed information from your group to the youth minister or other appropriate youth leader. Don't wait for them to ask. If you teach Sunday school, don't assume your students are going to other youth events. Passing along copies of your attendance records and any special needs you've noticed will help other leaders join you in keeping students from falling through the cracks.

Didjamissme? Respond to absentees. Nothing is worse than not being missed.

Care Enough *Not* to Send Hallmark Make your own "Missing You" cards. Take a class photo; have reprints made; and attach the photo to a computer-made or clip art designed colorful cardstock "card."

TEACHER/STUDENT'S HOME

A child identifies his parents with God, whether or not the adults want that role. —James Dobson

On the Road Again Arrange transportation for students who desire to attend but have no means to do so. Don't wait for students or parents to ask. Contact parents and work out an arrangement suitable for all involved.

Hot Topics Parents of teens may have qualms about their youth's participation in lessons on "hot topics" such as abortion or homosexuality. When planning a lesson on a sensitive topic, send parents a brief note: "Wednesday (date) our class will have a lesson on the topic of abortion. If you have concerns regarding this lesson, feel free to call me at (your phone number)." Your openness with parents is a must and they will appreciate your communication.

Spread the Good News Compliment your students *to* their parents.

El Dummo, Sir Teens have a tendency to think their parents are stupid. Moms and dads everywhere will love you for defending parents. When appropriate, you can connect points from the Scripture lessons to their own situations by saying something like, "See guys, you don't like it when your parents worry about the kind of girls you want to date. But look what happened to Samson!"

Mum's the Word Don't allow students to reveal things about their families which are too personal. Parents would not take kindly to finding out that their deepest secrets were part of a public discussion.

Apply at Home Some of your lessons should include suggestions that students can implement at home to improve student-parent relations: telling their parents they appreciate them, volunteering for extra chores, agreeing to do their regular chores without being nagged, and picking mom up from a dead faint when these things are actually done!

What a Concept Have times in class when teens pray for their parents. And let the parents know they are being prayed for.

Keep in Touch Occasionally communicate with students' parents by phone or postcard.

On the Home Front Find out about the home situation of each new student. This information will help you relate appropriately to your students. For example, consider that a child of divorced parents may only be able to attend every other week.

Road Trip When taking a road trip with students, give all needed information, release forms, etc. directly to parents. Don't assume that materials handed to students will ever be seen by their parents!

STUDENT/STUDENT

A faithful friend is an image of God.

Say Mozzarella! Stage a photo shoot of your class members. Choose a backdrop and coordinate colors of clothes to wear. Take several poses. Present each student with a photo of his choice. Use leftover photos to enclose with letters your class writes to TV producers complimenting or criticizing their shows, a local newspaper editor, or congress.

Mirror Kids If you have a Polaroid camera and a photocopier at church, take a photo of one student each week. Make photocopies for each class member. Instruct students to attach the picture to their mirrors at home and pray for the "Mirror Kid of the Week."

Tips for Teachers—Teens

News Reporter Let students take turns being the "News Reporter of the Day." The reporter should arrive early, greet each student, and make note of any accomplishments from the past week, prayer requests, etc. The reporter opens the class time with his broadcast: "Today's crime headline: Lisa killed the competition in the Regional Math Contest. In sports, James won the 3rd place wrestling award for Lakepoint High. Health news: Nikki is recovering from her tonsillectomy. And now, . . . back to you, Teach."

Personality Plus A lesson on personality traits is useful. This helps students analyze why they're attracted to certain people and not to others. A lesson with this focus also teaches that there are not "good" and "bad" types, but rather complementary strengths and weaknesses.

Fickle Friends Junior highers may be rather shallow, switching friends from week to week. If different students seem to be left out from time to time, don't make an issue of it. A problem arises when one student is continually the only one left out. Speak to some of the offenders privately: "I know Jackie isn't really your type; but she needs your influence."

Prayer Chain Start a telephone prayer chain just for your group. Deliberately mix up the order of calling so students must call those they don't know well.

Getting to Know You Social, fun times are important. Cleverly planned activities can be used to group students together with students not in their regular circle of friends. For example, if you are dividing into teams for a game, hand out two flavors of jawbreakers, being careful to give different flavors to those you know to be good friends. Then all "red tongues" form one team, and all "blue tongues" form the other.

Building Relationships

School Daze Students in your class may come from several different schools. Closeness may not come automatically. Friendship cannot be forced. But the common bond of Christ along with the comfortable atmosphere you create will soon produce friendships.

Pass the Basket Have students write their names on strips of paper. Fold the papers and drop them in a basket. As students leave, ask them to pick a name from the basket and pray for that person throughout the week.

Phony Facts For a fun getting-to-know-you icebreaker, ask each student to write down his name and three "facts" about himself. But one of the "facts" isn't true. For example, one teacher wrote:

1. I was once asked to be in a beauty contest.
2. I have a collection of Agatha Christie novels.
3. I gave up a scholarship to law school to attend Bible college.

Let each student read his "facts." The class must guess which fact is phony.

Break It Up For a lesson on racism or prejudice, divide the class into two unusual groups, such as blondes and brunettes or January-June and July-December birthdays. This makes the point well. Hard-line clique members will find it painful to sit with those outside their group.

Special-Tees Have a T-shirt design contest in your class or group and order special T-shirts from the winning design. Or order matching Christian message T-shirts from Living Epistles (1-800-635-3128) and have your own unique logo imprinted on the sleeve. Designate occasions when everyone will wear the shirts. Order extras to use as giveaways, for visitors, and for new members.

Tips for Teachers—Teens

A Pat and a Pen on the Back After your class members have gotten to know one another, plan this special activity. Attach a piece of colorful cardstock paper to a piece of yarn, making a necklace. Instruct students to hang these around their necks with the paper on their backs. Give students pens and tell them to write something encouraging on the back of every other student. Allow plenty of time—and be sure to participate as well.

Encouragement Via Postal Service Keep cards in your classroom to be signed and sent by your class.

TEENS WITH DISABILITIES

Alone we can do so little, together we can do so much. —Helen Keller

My Buddy Train teenagers to be buddies to their peers who have disabilities. Suggest specific ways to help: pushing a wheelchair, turning pages, assisting in feeding, or simply sitting with their friend during class or worship.

In His Steps Study the Bible to see how Jesus interacted with people with disabilities. Let students list His responses (i.e., compassion, acceptance, touch). Look at Psalm 139, Matthew 25:31-40 and Luke 14:7-24.

Career Day Hold a session in which teens will be introduced to the many careers open to them in Christian service with the disabled and their families. Have information—or a representative—available from colleges that prepare students for disability-related vocations.

Watch Me Model Christ-like responses to persons with disabilities. Teens will learn by your example, so it is super important for teachers and other adults to lead out in displaying patience, compassion, and tolerance.

Up Close and Personal Invite an adult with a disability to visit your class or group. After a brief, informal presentation, allow students to ask questions.

Volunteer Encourage teens to connect with community agencies that serve the disabled. Invite a representative of the Special Olympics to share with your students how they could be involved as coaches or assistants. Suggest that students volunteer for special programs offered through the local parks and recreation department. Support and encourage students as they reach out in this way.

Be Prepared Take time to prepare non-disabled students when you are aware a teen with a disability will be joining your class. Give details about their new friend's disability, any specialized equipment he uses, and how they might best be a friend.

Ask If you have a student with a disability and are unsure of his or her needs, *ask*.

Walk a Mile in My Shoes Use simulation activities to help sensitize students to the daily struggles faced by those with disabilities. Lead a session in which each of your students has to perform a series of daily tasks while blindfolded, in a wheelchair, or physically limited in some other way. Spend time debriefing after this session.

INTERGENERATIONAL

How old do you think you would be if you didn't know your age?

Focus on Senior Saints Challenge your class to host a senior saints luncheon, banquet, dessert, or after-Sunday-school coffee break. Let your students serve and mingle. Ask a local antique dealer to set up a display. Play music from "their" generation. Invite the local oldies car club to park their cars at the church entrance. Ask one of the older saints to share his or her pilgrimage of faith.

Elective Classes Occasionally give the opportunity to mix age groups for classes. Cooperate with other teachers to offer several electives. Allow everyone from junior high through senior saints to sign up for the thirteen-week elective of their choice.

God's Family Reunion Organize intergenerational activities: anything from all-church roller-skating to a "Pizza and Parables" evening at which all ages get together to act out assigned parables and feast on pizza after the performances.

I Remember When Invite an older "saint" to give a testimony or share a unique life experience with your class or group.

Buddy System Look for natural "buddies." Arrange for your student with a love of fishing to "hook up" with an older Christian with the same zeal.

On Tour If your class prepares a skit as a part of a lesson, arrange to have them perform it for several other classes.

Enlist Older Volunteers Many of today's kids have no grandmas or grandpas in their lives. Ask senior saints to be involved with your students in a variety of ways. Older people can add a dimension that may be missing in your students' lives—and vice versa.

Like a Child Volunteer your class to take over the nursery or beginner class one Sunday. Debrief later and discuss childlike faith.

Twelve to Eighteen If your class includes both junior and senior high students (which usually is not an ideal situation) you will need to be particularly creative in spanning the 12- to 18-year-old age range. Challenge older students to share their wisdom. For example, let seniors teach a lesson entitled "Everything I Wish I'd Known as a Christian Before Stepping Through the Doors of Jacksonville High School."

IDEAS FOR TEACHING

ATTENTION-GETTERS

> *Where my reason, imagination, or interest was not engaged, I would not and could not learn.*
> —*Winston Churchill*

Game Plan Make sure your lesson is set up to cover these three vital points:
1. Focus—getting students' attention
2. Discover—finding out what the Bible says
3. Respond—applying what is learned to daily life

Think Tabloid Use bizarre headlines to advertise an upcoming lesson. In Moses' song (Exodus 15:8), the water in the Red Sea is described as "congealed." Why not announce your lesson on the crossing of the Red Sea with the title "The World's Largest Jell-O?" Jacob's unfortunate marriage to Leah could be called "Honeymoon Over When the Lights Came On!" (A few parents may show up for this one!)

In a Flash Suddenly take a flash photo of your students, caught by surprise. Use this attention-getter to lead into a lesson on the second coming of Christ.

Mr. Potato Head Goes to Sunday School Bring in your favorite childhood toy (which may be sold in antique stores these days!). Use the toy as an object lesson to lead into a lesson on *childlike,* as opposed to *childish,* faith. Or use a "magic slate" toy to discuss God's "erasing" our sins when we ask forgiveness. Let students build with Lincoln Logs or Legos and then discuss the parable of the rich fool (Luke 12:13-21).

Scripture Scramble Edit a Scripture passage by replacing certain words with incorrect information. Let students "catch" each mistake and discuss. For example, Matthew 3:1 might read "In those days, *Jane* the Baptist came, preaching in the *malls* of Judea and saying, '*Repaint,* for the *democracy* of heaven is near.'"

Bible Rip Out Hide a piece of scrap paper in your Bible. When you are reading a particularly "difficult" Scripture, say, "I don't think I could possibly do that. I wish that wasn't in the Bible!" Pretend to rip out that page of your Bible, but really tear the scrap paper in two. This is guaranteed to get a reaction!

Green Card Make a creative version of a Christian "green card" (a visa permitting foreign nationals to work and reside in the United States). Pull this card from your wallet or billfold to begin a discussion centered on living as aliens in this world and having our true citizenship in heaven.

Tips for Teachers—Teens

Sunday Morning at the Movies Bring the weekend movie advertisement section from your newspaper. Allow kids to talk about movies they've seen and comment on the ads. Then read Philippians 4:8 and direct the discussion from the "think on these things" perspective.

BIBLE TEACHING METHODS

What criminals we are to let the Bible seem dull, commonplace, removed from life, when it is the very Word of Life.
—Lois LeBar

Model Jesus No . . . really. *Model* Jesus' love. During one entire class session, you and your whole class must concentrate on speaking and acting as Jesus would. Use Ephesians 5:1 as a verse to memorize.

Student Teacher Occasionally give willing students an opportunity to teach portions of your lesson.

Dress-Up Time Yes, in a *teen* class. Keep a costume box in your classroom. Act out a parable spontaneously, with appropriate "costuming." Then go down the hall and give a command performance for the 5-year-olds.

I Hear, I Forget. I See, I Remember Put Scripture to slides or video. Challenge students to think visually to create presentations on the armor of God (Ephesians 6:10-17), the body of Christ (1 Corinthians 12:12-31), or the sheep and the goats (Matthew 25:31-46).

Relevant to the Max **Make every lesson a Bible lesson. Don't separate the Bible from daily life. Emphasize in a variety of ways how the Bible applies to every area of life.**

Time Lines **Teens are able to put Bible chronology together.** Purchase contemporary Bible maps and time lines and display them. Then you can quickly point out time periods, geography, etc. during your lessons. Allow students to clip magazine photos that illustrate types of modern day behavior that mirror those of Bible times.

The Only Book God Ever Wrote Encourage students to bring their Bibles and use them during class. Don't spoon-feed the Bible to your students. Teach students basic Bible study skills (unless you plan to follow them around for the next sixty years!), and allow them the joy of discovering Bible truths on their own.

Who's Who in the Pew? **Make a chart of church ministries.** Instruct students to discover who chooses the songs for worship services, who mows the church lawn, who buys supplies for the nursery. See how the body of Christ works together. Study 1 Corinthians 12:12 and Romans 12:4. Challenge students to discover specific ways they can be an active part of the body.

Bumper Sticker Lesson Challenge your students to write down all the bumper sticker sayings (or T-shirt sayings) they see in one week. List them; then "debrief" biblically. For example, what would the Christian response be to "Whoever dies with the most toys wins?"

Road Trip! Who says all Bible learning has to take place between four walls and on cold metal chairs? Teach an Easter lesson in a cemetery. Studying the Ten Commandments? Have your lesson in a courtroom. Teach Hebrews 12:1 in a sports arena. Gather by a lake to hear about fishers of men.

Here Comes Da Judge Ask a judge, doctor, policeman, or other official to address your class on a pertinent topic.

How Was That Again? Use alliterations to retell familiar stories. For example, the parable of the wheat and tares might include this line: "Sit still, the supervisor suggested, since shoveling the scraggly stalks simultaneously snags the superior specimens."

Something New Under the Sun Your worst teaching method may be the one you use every week without fail. Try something new. Don't stick with the safe. Take a risk.

In Other Words Have students study the Bible passage at hand, then write a paraphrase. For example, a line from the rewritten prodigal son might read, "While he was on the road again, his old man spotted him and freaked out and made tracks to greet him. It was hug city and dad even laid one on him."

To Be Continued Develop an open-ended story. Set up the main characters and the situation; then let students decide the outcome.

Be a Prostitute For a witnessing lesson, let students take turns being the Christian witness while you role play the witnessee—a prostitute, convict, troubled friend, street person, executive.

Shake 'Em Up Play the devil's advocate to get a discussion fired up.

Lecture. Yes, Lecture Sometimes the most efficient method is a brief lecture. The operative word here is "brief." If you do lecture, the material should be boiled down into a dynamic mini-speech—not five minutes' worth stretched out to fill a twenty-minute hole in your lesson.

Give and Take Don't use discussion as a major teaching method on your first day of class. Junior highers in particular may shrivel at the mere thought. But after you have developed an atmosphere of openness and acceptance, discussion is a wonderful tool. When students share their ideas, others will see that their own thoughts are not so ridiculous. And as the teacher, hearing what kids say gives you insight into feelings, problems, etc. Just remember to come back to: "We've heard lots of interesting thoughts. Now we must balance our thoughts with what the Bible says."

The Sound of Silence Don't be afraid of a little silence.

Question and Answer Ask good questions. "Who died for our sins?" is not a good question for teens. They feel silly offering to answer a second grade question, and they'd be mortified if they should happen to answer an easy question incorrectly. Steer away from questions that can be answered with one word. Shoot for questions that ask "Why?" and "How?" and "So what?"

Ophree Sinfree Show Let your students host a talk show on a current topic. Invite a panel of guests, or let students take sides among themselves to create the discussion panel.

Version Variations Have students look up particular Scripture verses in more than one version of the Bible. For example, Colossians 3:5 in three versions reads:

"Mortify therefore your members which are upon the earth" (*KJV*).

"Put to death, therefore, whatever belongs to your earthly nature" (*NIV*).

"So put all evil things out of your life" (*ICB*).

Music

> *Music is a powerful medium. Music can be used as a vehicle for any passion. The music itself is only a tool. It opens the mind. But once you have opened the mind you must feed it.*
>
> —*Billy Ray Hearn, President, Sparrow Records*

Now Playing Have Christian music (cassette tape, CD, or video) playing in your room before class time. Display the jacket, song lyrics, or a poster of the musical group. This gives early arrivals an interest to focus on, as well as an introduction to the variety of Christian music available.

Music to Chew On Play a song that relates to your lesson topic as students enter. Use the song again in a more focused way during the lesson.

Special Request Ask the local Christian radio station to dedicate a song to your class at the designated time on Sunday morning. Use this song to introduce your class to the topic of the day.

A Real Deal A quarterly Christian music subscription service, interlínc (1-800-725-3300), provides the latest in Christian music, as well as Bible study materials based on God's Word and using songs from each of the cassettes, CDs, or videos.

Use Youth Talent Ask musically talented students to prepare a song on a specific upcoming topic.

But He Wears a Cross! And your students also heard him sing the words "God" and "prayer." Students who listen to secular music may misunderstand the use of "Christian sounding" words. Listen to songs with them and help them discern real meanings. Get information on the musicians' lifestyles to see if their lives line up with the "Christian sounding" words they sing.

See That Song Teach Scripture songs in sign language. Kids will remember the words as they concentrate on making the appropriate hand gestures.

Back to Bach Use classical music to set a mood. For a lesson on Psalm 23, play "Sheep May Safely Graze" from Bach's Cantata 208 to lead into prayer and reflection. If your lesson concerns Jesus calming the stormy sea, have Mussorgsky's "Night on Bald Mountain" or "Dialogue of the Wind and Sea" by Debussy blasting out of your room as students enter. (Check your local library for these selections).

Tune in to Scripture Use Scripture songs to memorize Scripture.

Curriculum With a Beat Many contemporary Christian musicians publish Bible study materials and programming resources to go along with their music.

I Give It an "8" Let kids review an album of the week or month.

Mood Music Have the theme from *Indiana Jones* playing to introduce your lesson on Bible archaeology. Incorporate the theme from *Jaws* into your lesson on Jonah. Use your imagination.

Sound Effects Surprise your students by using sound effects. Use a sound effects CD and a CD player with a remote to add an audio element to a lesson. For example, use the hidden remote to start a hammering sound effect just as a student begins reading about Noah building the ark.

VISUALS

It is estimated that we retain 10% of what we hear and 50% of what we see and hear.

Why Use Visuals?
1. Jesus did.
2. We live in a visual world.
3. Visuals create atmosphere, capture attention, hold interest, provide variety, clarify ideas.

Scene Stealer Keep your eyes open for movie video scenes that illustrate upcoming lesson topics. Show a specific clip to illustrate a point. *Video Movies Worth Watching: A Guide for Teens* (Veerman, David, editor. Grand Rapids: Baker Book House, 1992) is a helpful resource.

Don't Forget Visuals include objects, models, handouts, marker boards, maps, diagrams, charts, photographs, toys, etc.

Recycle Save the best of posters and other visual aids from used curriculum. Begin a simple art file with the basic categories: people, places, and things. Branch out from there. Trade with other teachers. Ask public school teachers for their castaways. Your local Christian bookstore might donate slightly damaged visuals or outdated publicity posters.

Humongous Books Check your local library for oversize books which contain large pictures and photographs on every subject imaginable. (Artists' renditions of angels and demons are fascinating!)

Do-It-Yourself Video Prepare your own creative video clips. Interview the church staff or leadership. Ask dynamic Christians to give their testimonies on videotape. Encourage kids to make their own music video or act out a Bible story or Bible-based story.

Look Up Don't just tack a poster up on any old wall. Attach it to the ceiling!

Who, Me? Remember that you, as the teacher, are a walking, talking, breathing audiovisual. Your life speaks before your words. Your students are watching to see what difference Jesus makes in your life.

Where in the World? Keep a globe in your classroom. Refer to specific places when discussing world events, missionary prayer requests, etc.

Parts Are Parts Take photos of just the eyes, ears, noses, hands, etc. of your class members. Then put together a wild poster based on 1 Corinthians 12:12.

Always in Sight Teach from your Bible. Keep it in sight. It is your text, your curriculum, and your constant visual.

Done-for-Ya Video Edge TV (1-800-616-EDGE), a video magazine, is a series of videotapes on a variety of topics done creatively and especially for teens. Segments vary in length from two minutes to fifteen minutes. Segments stand alone and a discussion guide is included.

APPLICATION

> *There is absolutely no credit with the Lord for learning Bible facts apart from application and obedience. The Pharisees were the most knowledgeable people of their day in Scripture, and were the hardest group for Jesus to reach.* —**Dick Alexander**

Servin' Safari If you're wrapping up a series on service, plan a "Servin' Safari." Organize a canned good scavenger hunt; then deliver the goods to those in need. Package up used curriculum to send to missionaries who desire it. Help Habitat for Humanity build a house. Build a wheelchair ramp for your church. Serve—somehow.

Missionary Connection Adopt a missionary and send cards, photos, and cassette or video greetings.

Put Legs on Lessons If you teach "Love your neighbor," for heaven's sake, find some neighbors to love! Plan to serve at a soup kitchen, write letters to prisoners, or collect canned goods or winter coats. One teacher called his class early one winter morning and instructed them to wear boots and bring a shovel to Sunday school. Their "lesson" consisted of shoveling sidewalks for elderly folks.

Bible McNuggets Somewhere in each lesson, try finding one nugget of truth that students can apply to their lives immediately. Make sure your students have grasped the key "McNugget" of each lesson.

Class Project Consider supporting a needy child with class offerings, or "adopting" a local nursing home or children's rehabilitation center where ongoing relationships can be formed.

This Week in My Life Use illustrations from your own life to build bridges from God's Word to daily activities.

SCRIPTURE MEMORY

I have hidden your word in my heart that I might not sin against you (Psalm 119:11, NIV).

Personalized Scripture Insert students' names in Scripture passages, such as "For God so loved Tina Rumsey that he gave his one and only Son" (John 3:16), or "No temptation has seized Ryan Henry except what is common to man" (1 Corinthians 10:13). Ask someone who does calligraphy to design a bookmark or other keepsake with each student's personalized Scripture verse on it.

Scripture Melodies Incorporate choruses taken directly from Scripture into lessons and activities.

Ooze Method Have students write a Scripture verse on a Post-it Note. Instruct them to attach the Post-its to their mirrors at home, and let the verse "ooze" into their lives.

Tips for Teachers—Teens

Doodle a Verse Let students draw stick figures, cartoons, or just plain doodle to illustrate a chosen Scripture verse.

Scripture by Beat Put Scripture verses to beat. For example, can you snap your fingers and hear the beat in this verse? "Trust in the Lord with all your heart and lean not on your own understanding; in all your ways acknowledge him, and he will make your paths straight" (Proverbs 3:5, 6, *NIV*).

It's a Natural Become so immersed in Scripture that it becomes a natural part of conversation and discussion. Students will remember Scripture that makes sense in context of real life situations.

SEASONAL IDEAS

If Christianity does not make a man happy, it will not make him anything at all . . . . Christianity is the faith of the happy heart and the shining face.
—William Barclay

Blast Off "Launch" your promotees with a lesson focused on their career goals. Find out what your students think they'd like to pursue vocationally. Bring in library books and other information on those areas of interest. Let the rest of the class chip in to help present ways your promotees could start working toward their goals. Discuss how each career could please the Lord.

Graduation Teach a special "seniors series" for graduating seniors.

Promotion Day Promotion Day is a good day to remind your promotees to wear their spiritual armor (Ephesians 6:10-17) as they continue to grow spiritually.

Con-Grad-ulation Gifts Instead of giving a gift to college-bound graduates in May or June, wait until August and give them a devotional book to take to college and begin as school begins.

Stump the Teacher Day If you end up with a short lesson, have a "Stump the Teacher Session." Students may ask any Bible question or they may fill in "I'll bet the Bible doesn't say anything about _____." You must answer. This is great fun and quite enlightening for all!

Celebrate Silly Days Buy a calendar of unique days to celebrate. Or look for *Chase's Annual Events: The Day-by-Day Directory to (year)* (Chicago: Contemporary Bks., Inc.) in the reference section of your local library. Then celebrate!

Decorate a Door Some students might enjoy decorating their classroom door seasonally, or to promote a current or upcoming topic of study.

THE CLASSROOM

Your classroom speaks before you do.

Bulletin Board Buddy Beware of yellowed bulletin boards! If you don't have time to keep classroom bulletin boards up-to-date, recruit someone who isn't called to teach, but would be glad to design a new board every quarter.

Polish the Dull Side Make the most of the room you have. If you can't see the bright side, polish the dull side.

About Face Even if there's not much you can do to change your room, remember that something as simple as facing a different wall can feel new.

Home Sweet Home Give students some ownership of the room, if possible. Let their personalities show.

Clorox Commandos What are we going to do until dark, moldy classrooms are outlawed? Do your best to create a bright, airy, clean teaching environment. If your room is . . . uh, nasty, have a class work day. Let your "Clorox Commandos" give it their best shot. Follow the cleaning with a pizza party during which you design your ideal classroom. Remind your students that if your present class size would grow enormously (hint, hint) you would have to move to a bigger (and hopefully, better) room!

The Classroom

Christian Graffiti/"E-vandalism" Let the students paint one wall of their classroom any way they want. Suggest Scripture verses, Christian slogans, phrases from Christian songs, artwork, and perhaps a theme. But remember, it doesn't matter if you think it's ugly, because it's *their* wall.

Mood Lighting Create "moods" by using candles, strobes, darkness, or a colored spotlight on a particular object.

Living Things Liven up your room with plants, an aquarium, or something else that is alive and speaks of our Creator.

Reading Material Place current issues of Christian teen magazines (i.e., *Brio, Breakaway, Campus Life*) in your classroom.

Well Supplied Make sure your classroom isn't learning impaired by its lack of supplies and resources.

Lending Library Set up a checkout corner where students can borrow Christian music CDs, cassettes, or videos, Christian novels, and biographies of Christians who made a difference.

THE TEACHER'S SPIRITUAL AND MENTAL PREPARATION

A teacher affects eternity; he can never tell where his influence stops.
—Henry Adams

Motive Teach for the Lord. Don't expect thanks.

Focus Commit each session to the Lord.

Prepare to Learn Thoroughly prepare to teach a first-rate lesson each week. But don't forget to enter the class session with the anticipation of what you might learn. *To teach is to learn twice.* —Joseph Joubert

Team Teach It may seem like you're teaching alone, but rest assured, the Holy Spirit is team teaching God's Word with you.

So Whadayado? When you are at a social gathering and someone asks, "And what do you do?," do you answer by telling them about your 9-to-5 job? If teaching is a top priority for you—and we know it is—then say so. Try this next time: "Well, the most important thing I do is teach junior high Sunday school." The reactions are fun to watch.

Heart Check Read 1 Corinthians 13:1-3. What is your motivation for teaching? Guilt, duty, or "if I don't do it, who will?" *Love* is the only pure motivation.

The Enemy Will Attack The devil hates spiritual growth in God's children. He will attempt to sabotage anything that could advance God's Kingdom of light. Don't forget.

A Precious Soul Each of your students is a soul for whom Christ died. Teach them with that in mind.

Get an Attitude—An Eternity Attitude What you do is "wrapped in eternity." God expects something to happen when His Word is taught. It could change the course of history for a young person.

Get Re-Charged Attend a teacher training day or convention.

Take a Hike—Through a Christian Bookstore, That Is. Carry a notepad and pen and jot down ideas, curriculum resources, song titles, and ideas that you might be able to plug into lessons.

Your Calling You are called to obedience, not success.

Furnish Your Mind Subscribe to Christian teen magazines, such as *Brio, Breakaway,* and *Campus Life* or youth worker magazines like *Group, Youth Worker's Update,* or *Parents of Teenagers.*

Can't Give Away What You Don't Have Keep in mind that your students will remember *you* long after the lesson topic fades. Get your heart right before teaching theirs.

Give Up That's right. *You* can't do it. But God working through you, can (Philippians 4:13, Ephesians 3:20).

LESSON PREPARATION

Good teachers are not born; they are made by conscientious labor.
—*Henrietta Mears*

Have a Plan, Stan Whether you use published curriculum or your own unique plan, map your lesson out. Know where you're going in the lesson and how you are going to get there.

Reality Check Your students need real answers to real questions. Your preparation is vital in order to equip your young people.

Time Is Precious Thirty minutes of lesson time, fifty-two weeks a year is only twenty-six hours. That's barely a full day of intensive Bible study during a whole year. You won't want to waste a single minute. Plan accordingly.

Be Flexible Don't over prepare your lesson to the point of rigidity.

Don't Assume When preparing, don't *assume* your students know the basics—Bible chronology, steps to salvation, books of the Bible, Bible heroes, etc. Better to briefly explain than to make wrong assumptions. And asking doesn't always help, because some students don't want to admit that they are fifteen years old and think the Epistles are the wives of the Apostles.

Lesson Preparation

Absentee Teacher When you must be absent on short notice, there isn't time for a substitute teacher to prepare a lesson, even if the substitute has a spare copy of your materials. A better idea is for your substitute teacher to have a book of extra lessons. Then your sub can have a quality standby lesson prepared at all times.

Think Ahead If you have a lesson on a sensitive topic, you may need to preplan your wording.

You Are Creative The question is "how creative?" Jump start your creativity by spending time with teachers you consider ultra-creative. *I not only use all the brains I have but all the brains I can borrow.* —Woodrow Wilson

Read Read current magazines and newspapers with a highlighter and/or scissors in hand.

No Christianese Allowed If you come upon "Christianese" while preparing a lesson, substitute kid-friendly words for abstract terms, such as sanctification, justification, righteousness, idolatry, countenance.

One Thing Set one major goal to be attained during your lesson. But make sure it is valid and that you get it across in a variety of ways. Know your goal. If you aim at nothing, you're bound to hit it.

Time to Incubate Read your lesson materials early in the week, and allow time for incubation. You'll be surprised at how many "life experiences," newspaper articles, etc. will fit into your lesson plan as the week progresses.

Know Thine Equipment Understand how to use a VCR before all eyes are focused on a blank TV screen!

Carry a "Wait" Bag Unexpectantly stuck in a waiting room? Not to fear! Redeem the time by pulling out your lesson from your "wait" bag.

Teach People, Not Curriculum Keep "your kids" in mind as you prepare your lesson. Ask yourself, "How is the topic relevant to Justin, Nick, Erica, Brandi, and Misty, today?"

Get Your Ducks in a Row Gather needed materials in advance. Don't go on a supplies scavenger hunt two minutes before class is to begin.

No Spoons Allowed Consider how you can provide your students with ways to participate in the lesson. Don't spoon-feed Bible information to them.

Illustrate Plan appropriate illustrations, such as "When I gave blood this week . . . ," or "At the football game . . . ."

DISCIPLINE

Our Father, keep us at tasks too hard for us that we may be drawn to you for strength.

—From a prayer carried by Eleanor Roosevelt in her purse

Uh-Ten-Shun! What is "paying attention," exactly? Your definition of paying attention may have to be altered when young teens are involved. They truly seem to have trouble making eye contact for long periods of time (especially in a small room). If you allow them to doodle or drink hot chocolate (rather than harping on them to pay attention) you may find that they relax. When relaxed, it may be less of a problem to "pay attention."

Be the Adult Do everything you can to stay in control and make the discipline positive and constructive.

Blast to the Past Even though teens want to be treated like adults, sometimes they are very childish. If a session starts getting out of hand, have a "blast to the past" break. Let them jump up and down, dance around, do the hokey-pokey . . . whatever they want to do to act like little kids for thirty seconds.

Because I Said So Be specific. Don't call kids down for "no apparent reason."

Anti-Whining Device **Head off discipline problems by using creative complaining. Any student who has a complaint must voice that complaint, using these three steps.**

1. State the complaint.
2. State your perception of the best solution.
3. State the part that you personally will play in effecting that solution.

Catch 'Em Being Good **Praise good behavior.**

Lay Down the Law **If you have set boundaries and communicated them to students, then if they have to be sent out of class, they have sent themselves.**

Follow Through **Don't threaten kids to within an inch of their lives and never take action. Keep your word. Be consistent.**

Private Matters **When the situation allows, call the student aside and deal with the problem privately.**

Look Deeper **Remember that bad behavior often masks a deeper cry for attention or help.**

Realistically Speaking **Some discipline problems might stem from unrealistic expectations on your part. For example, don't expect 13-year-olds to act like 18-year-olds. Ask yourself: "Are my rules and boundaries realistic; and are my students definitely aware of them?"**

Hush **Start you lesson in a whisper.**

Focus That Impulse **Put excess energy to work.**

Help Yourself **Teach relevant topics lovingly. If your class is interesting, meets needs, and your students feel cared for, discipline problems will be minimal.**

EVALUATION

Honest criticism is hard to take,
particularly from a relative, a friend, an
acquaintance, or a stranger.
—Franklin P. Jones

On a Scale of 1 to 10 Once a year, let the students evaluate your class. Some curricula include an evaluation form, or create your own. Ask students to rate the class on a scale of 1 to 10. What's their favorite thing about the class? What would they like to change? Copies of this should be passed on to the director of Christian education or other appropriate leader. (If you fear having a student evaluation, your teaching may need some fine-tuning).

Drop In Invite the director of Christian education, youth minister, or another teacher you respect to drop in *any time* to evaluate your class.

Parent Participation Invite parents of your students to sit in. You shouldn't need advance notice as far as preparation goes—you should be teaching a top-notch lesson weekly. But advance notice would be nice so the adult visitors don't outnumber the regular students.

Evaluate Yourself What's working? What isn't? What haven't I tried? How's my attitude?

Tips for Teachers—Teens

Suggestion Box Use a suggestion box for the students to suggest topics, ask sensitive questions, constructively criticize, and give honest feedback.

Be Flexible It's not the end of the world if you don't "finish the lesson," *if* something better happens. And you'll know when it does.

Ask Yourself Would I like being a student in my class?

AGE CHARACTERISTICS AND IMPLICATIONS FOR TEACHING

You were never his age—because the culture and issues change with each year and generation. Yes, some things are basic, but how they are handled and lived out is different for every generation.

—Gary B. Zustiak,
Professor of Youth Ministry,
Ozark Christian College

IMPLICATIONS FOR TEACHING YOUNG TEENS

A. The young teen years are fertile for spiritual growth. Young teens are often more interested in spiritual matters than they let on outwardly.

B. Young teens need to be guided—not pushed.

C. Challenge young teens and give them opportunities for service.

D. Allow them to make choices.

E. Use positive peer pressure to your advantage.

F. Offer social activities in a positive Christian environment.

G. Accept them. Try not to be easily shocked.

H. Be patient.

I. Have lots of fun. Laugh *with* young teens, not *at* them.

J. Young teens need lots of upbuilding relationships with people of varying ages.

K. Always make connections between faith and daily life. Young teens want a faith that applies to their lives *now*.

L. Remember that kids are becoming older at younger ages.

M.Prepare young teens for leadership by offering more and more bite-sized responsibilities.

N. Don't underestimate the value of Christian adults in the development of young adolescents.

Young Teen Age Characteristics

—Testing independence while desiring to belong

—Wants to serve meaningfully

—Experiencing tremendous physical changes

—Capable of abstract thinking

—Wants logical reasons

—Determining self concept

—Developing own faith

—Awakening sexually

—Self-conscious

—Post-child, pre-adult

—Influenced by peers

—Fluctuating emotions

—Has active imagination

—Good sense of humor

Illustrated by Keith Locke

Older Teen Age Characteristics

—Strong desire for independence

—Worries about purpose in life

—Has definite interests in skills

—May have complex life

—Music is second language

—Pressured to conform

—Feels stress

—Sexually aware

—Wants to succeed

—May be lonely

—Settling on own
value system

—Wants to belong
and feel secure

Illustrated by Keith Locke

Implications for Teaching Older Teens

A. Present a faith that makes a contribution to teens' lives *today*.

B. Offer a safe environment for expressing doubts and asking questions.

C. Equip students to make decisions based on biblical teaching.

D. Don't confuse your students' grown-up bodies with emotional maturity.

E. Listen.

F. Offer lots of positive social activities set in a Christian environment.

G. Help students develop caring relationships with people of all ages.

H. Make sure ministry to teens is done *with* them, not *to* them.

I. Present consistent adult role models of the Christian faith.

J. Give older teens meaningful responsibilities.

K. Be aware that many teens' lives are shaped by a materialistic, pleasure-oriented, high-tech, depersonalized world.

L. Remember that a large percentage of students who graduate from high school, having never made a commitment to Christ, *never will*.